Social Studies

Social Studies

POETRY AS HISTORY, ETHICS, AND JOURNALISM

POEMS BY

STANLEY KUSUNOKI

Polaris
Publicattions
An impirint of
North Star Press of St. Cloud Inc.
www.NorthStarPress.com

ISBN:978-1-68201-155-3

First Edition

Printed in the United States of America

Published by Polaris Publications,
an Imprint of North Star Press of St. Cloud Inc.
www.NorthStarPress.com

In memory of my parents,

Kiyoshi and Pearl Kusunoki.

Table of Contents

SHARED HISTORIES
Why I Sing... 3
Green Card Voices Speak............................ 4
Pakuks.. 5
22nd Floor, Grenfell.................................. 6
A Street Tour in Belfast.............................. 7
Evensong 8
Once Again, the Children Lead 9
The Statue in New York Harbor 11
April 15, 2019.. 12
Wayside 13
Write Your Own Ending 14
Stock Photo 15
Choices 16
Concert at the Mayo Clinic 17
Refugees 18
Wait a Minute 19
Woodstock/ Come From Away 20
"I Can't Breathe" 22
Bible Study.. 24
Protest at Line 3 25
Smudged... 26
Winona Speaks 27
Paranoia—Driving Home After the Protest 28
Photos in the Paper.................................. 30
Video Clips 33
No Quarter.. 35
PERSONAL HISTORIES
A French Requiem 39
Old School... 40
Queen Street Dublin: A Short Story 41
If Only, or (Un) Intended Consequences 43

Ode to Mary Oliver...............................45
Mary Becomes the Evening......................46
Au Revoir 47
Our Johnny, We Hardly Knew Ye 49
Night Wanderings 50
First Fall, January 2019...........................51
The Second Fall... 52
The Valley Path 53

FUTURE HISTORIES

Failure 56
Grandma 58
The Painful Truth 59
The Art and Science of Humanity 60
Soup 67
Uncertain 68
When I'm Lost.....................................70
When I was a Butterfly............................72
When He Asks.....................................74
In Came a Bus From Idaho 76
What They Forget About Hubris.................78

ACKNOWLEDGEMENTS

SHARED
HISTORIES

Why I Sing...

It's definitely not about ability
I open my mouth and what comes out
can be a lemon forgotten
in back of the fridge for months
Or a perfectly fresh rosé wine sipped
on the stoop
Saturday afternoon passing before us

It's about harmonic change
Sending my voice out to mingle
with other songs
All our spirits hearing themselves
called forward
Each breath, each stanza
clears the lungs,
cleanses the mind
Leaving hearts open
Communion

<u>Green Card Voices Speak</u>

Suburban kids assembled
For some, a first-time experience
You can see their wondering looks
Questioning eyes
Generations from their
Immigration story

But others'
—lives unfolding
from strangers
Who could be their brothers,
Sisters, cousins
The power of words
Validation:
"We are not terrorists,
Not leaches sucking the lifeblood
Of America
But the future promise
Making America great again
In the eyes of the world."

Pakuks

Note: In Anishinaabe folklore, Pakuks are the flying bones of dead children.

In *The Birchbark House*, a children's book,
Louise Erdrich tells us of pakuks—
Flying bones visited
late night fires in winter.
Anishinaabe elders holding their listeners
in rapt attention against the real windigos
of the season of long nights

These days they visit me in nightmares
Each time children die from a gun—
Sandy Hook, Columbine,
Marjory Stoneman Douglas, Uvalde—
Rattling bones invade my sleep
"Why did you let this happen?" screams
the midnight wind
"You have arms and legs
to make a change
You have a voice to add
to voices we carry
in our whirlwind travels
Do not be one who sits and frets
and blames the gunslingers
We will haunt your waking hours
All of us children
dead because of your inaction
We will fly through your denial
unrelenting
We have nowhere else to go
We will swirl by your side,
filling your hollow psyche
until you act."

22nd Floor, Grenfell

You will discover
the blackened bones of my mother
covering in futility
my baby sister's charred remains
But you will not find me—
A pile of nothing

A business expense
in the loss and gains columns
Cheap siding maximizing profits
Replaceable

My mum's meager wages mean
cutting the margins
The expense of sprinklers,
requests for
lighted hallways,
fire escapes
Just so much noise
interrupting the slumbers of landlords

A Street Tour in Belfast

"Ah Da, you're taking them on the death and destruction tour..."
-Seamus' younger son, Michael

"It's best you don't say my name here,"
says Seamus,
on the Orange side of the "Peace Wall"
He knows
the air is still buzzing
from street riots
just three days past

He shows us which bars
are patronized by which faction
Who is in control
of each intersection
Barbed fences
and murals on brick walls—
"You cannot get away from the troubles."

This scene confounds
the students in my reading class—
Why are all the sons and daughters
of Abraham constantly at war?
Cousins, even fathers and sons—
Violence to each other
Both sides claiming Jesus as their own

Evensong

Camilla dries the last of the dishes
Seamus sits down at the piano
Plays and sings an Irish folksong
An invitation?
I pick up Michael's out-of-tune guitar,
listen for the base chord,
re-tune, and join in
to Seamus' surprised delight

An Irish-raised survivor of the troubles
A Midwestern Japanese-American
share the same songbook,
weaving harmonies
like old singing buddies—
spotting each other a solo

In the midsummer gloaming
we are still reveling in song and camaraderie

Back home, Claudia will say
Of all the moments that shine
it was this time of shared music
Summer sunset at our backs
into the twilight
Lingering, the last chord

Once Again, the Children Lead

Sixteen-year-old
sails the North Atlantic
while we shuffle hands in pockets
Who should have made her ocean voyage moot
Mute as the corpses of dinosaurs
and zooplankton
that fuel the changes threatening her world
and ours

Her sea change challenge:
"Coal? So nineteenth century
Oil? So fifties"
Greta and her posse say
While we
check our retirement funds,
clutch for golden 'chutes
Hedge, hedge, hedge
our children's future

"I have a dream," Greta says
And it is Martin Luther King big—
Bold as the vision from the mountaintop
"I have a dream," Greta says
And the world's youth
understand
grown-ups pissing and moaning
about territory,
about settlements,
about "whose side are you on",
Is only so much bullshit

Social Studies

It matters for a second in the big picture
In the big picture
The waters are rising

And so are Greta and Gabriella
And Kiyoko and Sasha
And Hasan and Timon
Gaston, Juan and Gina

Each rising
Taking it to the streets
To the doors of the dinosaurs
Holding their lumps of coal

The Statue in New York Harbor

Needs a bath
Even the incoming
Irish immigrant can see
"Ah man, she's covered full o' seagull shite"

Humiliated, she winces
for her adopted country
"E Pluribus Unum" no longer
Just "unum"
Everyone "me first"

She covers her face
with her dimming torch
as the steps of democracy
are trampled by a mob,
drowning out cries for peace
With swastikas on their arms,
and semi-automatic rifles
brandished high

She prays for a torrential
rain of outrage against
the hate and division
to cleanse the country
Rinsing her face, her gown
Polishing the words at her feet
So that once again
she can raise her head
and proclaim her name
without feeling like a lie

April 15, 2019

Notre Dame is burning
Roof timbers from forests
remembered by ghosts
Smoke and ash, equalizers of class

Notre Dame is burning
The boundaries of rafter and roof
open now and spirits contained
in nave and sacristy
come and go like pigeons

Notre Dame is burning
The old song singed,
but stone walls and buttresses
save the stained glass rose

Remember
In the holiest of weeks
Notre Dame is burning
with a song of resurrection

Wayside

Out in the middle of nothing
Deciduous forest transitioning
to boreal conifers,
anxious driver spots the blue
highway sign of relief
A place to piss,
but also pause—

Why this place?
Carefully placed
stones mark the names of those dead
in disputes unresolved by reason

Ho-Chunk sacred ground perhaps
now re-sanctified
Away from the rush of traffic
under August twilight
Ghosts whisper
Stop, breathe
Listen to the stories we have to tell.

Write Your Own Ending

Because of a phone call
A fearful view of Islam

Because of a fearful view of Islam
The real terror goes ignored

Because the real terror goes ignored
Nineteen more children dead at school

Because of nineteen more children dead at school
Schools lock doors

Because of locked doors
Children learn fear

Because children learn fear
They do not become leaders

Because there are no leaders
Well, write your own ending

Stock Photo

He has become a stock photo
A poster-image for the border
The man drowned on the Texas bank of the Rio Grande
Prone in the mud, dead baby girl wrapped in his shirt
Where are they from? Guatemala?
Honduras, Venezuela?

He took the gambler's pick
The wager lost

The man who should care
Who should be the nation's conscience,
blames the dad
Blames all those waiting
at the border
Blames former Presidents
He dances stiff-legged
A Gestapo goose step
Replacing the two-step Texas style

<u>Choices</u>

Officer Yanez said he had no choice
Pulled the trigger

The jury said the same
Acquitted him of murder

Of course, there were choices
Choices to think beyond black and blue
The choice was to think, period.

Fear
Now there's a word
not spoken in the American Dream
Our promise
obliterated by a single word

Fear
erases everything
So that here,
not Chicago,
not Dallas,
not East St. Louis,

But here
on this turf,
a good and gentle man
is gone away

"It should have taken only one death,"
Says Fear
"You underestimate me at your peril—
As long as I am the motivator
You have no choice."

Concert at the Mayo Clinic

Piano music fills the Gonda Building atrium
Enthralled, we look over the railing
And there,
blue scrubs clad—
A nurse?
Intern?
Plays a waltz on the baby grand

Young woman sways
wanting to dance
Maybe self-conscious?
Feet tap, but legs wooden

Too bad
Dancing is good
Release from whatever,
whoever,
brought us all here
But see? She smiles still swaying
The music falls like snowflakes
Drifting her face

Refugees

The sermons focus
on the baby Jesus
Joseph and Mary

Migrants to Bethlehem
without shelter
now after Herod's decree,
Refugees
Which begs the question

What if Egypt had had a wall?
As in "Egypt first"
And "Make the Pharaohs
Great Again"
And border guards,
a Mideastern I.C.E.
chanting "No Jews!
Go back where you came from"

What then for the little family
Stopped at the border,
placed in detention
by Herod's men?
The Messiah's life cut short
No crucifixion
No resurrection
No Easter
No Christmas

What then?

Wait a Minute

Hold on now
Back in 1776
folks were pissed off
because the King
ignored their issues
Made orders
over the heads of governors
Made appointments without approval
Threatened anyone
who voiced opposing opinions
Tried to shut down the press
Took actions threatening
the welfare of coming generations

And what was their response?
Just asking

Woodstock/ Come From Away

Two different events
Separated by thirty years
Different players,
different setting
but sharing spirit

First
Half a million youngsters
crowd a farmer's field—
a commercial happening
turned into an open celebration
Organizers giving in to big hearts
No billy club bouncers
No armed guards
The barriers came down
instead of going up

Even when the rains came
turning farmer Yasgur's fields
into an amphitheater of mud,
people found ways
to make joy instead of frustration

And when the food was gone,
the outnumbered townspeople
sent groceries
made sandwiches

Now I wonder
Where in America
would a small town respond
like the people of Bethel
in these days of shutting doors?

Then, thirty years later
A great act of terror
sends thirty-eight airliners
to a hunk of basalt
on the fringe of Canada
A town, maybe nine thousand folks
with seven thousand instant guests
who have nowhere to go

No TSA
No metal detectors
Just humans
acting like humans

And like Woodstock,
music becomes the binding cloth
Language barriers erased
by song and dance
A common hymn
A common prayer
Lifted to the same God

And now I wonder
Where in America
would a small town respond
like the people of Gander
in these days of "Send them back"?

"I Can't Breathe"

What is it you don't understand
about "I can't breathe"?
Doesn't take a genius—
You can't breathe,
you die

When a guy says,
"I can't breathe"
and you are a human being,
you help
You're a cop—
you got a guy in a choke hold,
you got a knee on a neck
You lighten up,
unless your intent is murder

What is it you don't understand
about "I can't breathe"?
Doesn't matter he did a crime or not
You can't breathe,
you die

You take a breath yourself
Give it up
Your job—keep the peace
Not start a riot,
not burn the city,
not be prosecutor
judge and jury

What is it you don't understand
about "I can't breathe"?
Doesn't take Mother Theresa
to know you don't breathe,
you die

Doesn't matter you know this dude
from whatever past
or not
He says, "I can't breathe"
Your intent
for eight minutes
forty-eight seconds—
Murder to the Nth degree

Bible Study

He holds the book up
like he is hawking a box of cereal
Like it is his personal book—
A photo op for a publication party
Except,
he has just tear gassed,
and flash bombed,
shot rubber bullets
at the least of these
Jesus's brethren
So he can primp and pose,
show himself to be holy
He who has not cracked open the book,
much less understood its wisdom

He holds the book up
like it will shield him
from the sins he has wreaked upon the world
As if it will invoke forgiveness
for fouling the air,
poisoning the water
Allowing the pandemic to rebirth itself
Letting the moneychangers overrun the temple

He holds the book up,
but nobody is fooled
A prop, a bit of costume jewelry
He holds the book up

Protest at Line 3

The River molds itself to the earth
Twisting and turning
within the embrace of the land—
One and the other
Inseparable

But here, where the waters run
wild and clear,
the trees weep
in sorrow and anger
Their tribe ripped away
by the heart roots—
Torn from mother loam
A gash across the landscape

Open wound
in service to a new kind of artery—
A vessel without life-giving water,
but the crushed and condensed bodies
of zooplankton and algae
Forced out of their resting place
The liquid undead
pumped across sacred land
What need for this zombie flowage
in a time of diminishing return?
What need here where the risk is great?
Unholy blood
desecrates the earth
if even one drop is shed.

Smudged

The tobacco is honored
and set smoking
It caresses my face
Wafting over my head, a shroud
Not of death,
but of new life

It is done
I am no longer
an observer
I am a participant
Part of the spirit that binds
us to this place

Winona Speaks

Winona speaks,
and the river pauses
to let the words flow
across its surface
Trees stop their whispering
and grackles, sparrows, nuthatches
still their chatter
Redtail glides closer
to catch the words

Why is it
All of nature hears,
but we, who waste the land,
remain steadfast in our deafness?

Paranoia—Driving Home After the Protest

Here we are
Two brown bodies
leaving alone
after the main body of pilgrims
has departed
Two sets of headlights
in tandem southward
into the gloaming

A glance in the mirror
reveals a a third car following—
White Dodge Charger,
light bar on the roof,
the mark of the county sheriff
"What are the odds?"
I wonder as I slow
below the posted speed limit
Perhaps he will pass

He does not
He traces our passage
round each curve,
neither gaining nor receding
Should I worry?
Nothing done wrong,
but too many newspaper stories,
too many television reports

It is a long way
When I turn,
my friend Christian following behind me turns
and the cruiser continues on its course

SHARED HISTORIES

I imagine Christian sighing in his VW
I exhale,
move up to the speed limit
Heading home

Photos in the Paper

1. Insurgent breaking into the Capitol with a confederate flag

Inside the Capitol of the United States
A confederate flag
carried by one who would Make America
Great Again

What America does he imagine?

His own
America
Not ALL the people,
just the people who think like him
Who for all their bravado,
are acting out of fear

Fear that outnumbered,
they will be treated the same way
as the poor are treated
As the immigrant—
As anyone with skin darker than alabaster

2. Insurgent beating Capitol Policeman with an American flag

Excuse me?
Hello?
I want to ask a question
Yes, you brandishing the flag like a weapon
What are you thinking?
I want to know

Because I don't understand
how what you are doing
makes America better
How you are protecting freedom?

3. Capitol Assistants Carry the Ballot Boxes to Safety

Here are heroes
Not members of Congress
Or Capitol security
Young women—pages?
Carry the chests of ballots
Down the hallway
Eyes focused, counting the steps

4. Congressman Andy Kim cleans the Capitol floor

After the mayhem,
here is Andy Kim
by himself,
picking up broken glass
Shards prick his hands,
but the pain is in his heart
How this could happen
anywhere in America,
but especially here?
He wonders
if this place can be restored
to its intended state

5. Capitol Police Drawing the Flag Down to Half-Mast

A long shot during the aftermath
The Capitol roof
Police lower the flag
for fallen comrades
Does the frenzied hoard
comprehend that they have committed murder?

Video Clips

It is hard to imagine
Just two weeks
after the desecration,
the Capitol is ready to celebrate
a new President

We have the TV on all day
Tuned to PBS
and we are not disappointed

Between the pundits' interpretations
Video clips show:
Lady Gaga looking up
at the Capitol dome
during her performance of
The National Anthem
Yes,
the flag is still there

Amanda Gorman
takes it to the world
Poetic wisdom,
truth,
and youthful energy
to propel us forward

A firefighter, Andrea Hall,
leads the Pledge of Allegiance

Even Garth Brooks
taking off his hat to sing
"Amazing Grace"

Social Studies

Former Presidents
join the new President
at the Tomb of the Unknowns

It goes on and on
into the evening
And in the fireworks glow,
we realize
this,
all this,
is what we have been missing

The pageantry,
the ceremonies,
symbolizing
This country is vaster
than one man's vision
More complex and varied
than one man's tweets

But all of us
becoming the addends,
compiling strengths,
acknowledging weaknesses
Joining voices and hearts
To work for a more perfect union

No Quarter

The virus has been lurking
Waiting for the heartbreak moment
Its timing is perfect
Doesn't matter if I'm infected
or not,
it just laughs
Another dinner date ruined
Another connection quashed
Another chance for face-to-face
Now face down

Oh, the virus is an opportunist
Laughs hysterically
as face mask denier,
cleric, lies in hospital bed
begging for prayers

You need more than
intercession from God
You who fail to follow
the God that is biology

No, I will pray for your
congregation,
but not for you
That's between you
and the entity you swore
to honor and obey
Between you
and the one who gives,
and takes life away

PERSONAL HISTORIES
Elegies and Observations

A French Requiem

I got the news Madame Mourre died,
and it's like a summer cloud passing
I was thinking about it all
while eating ratatouille, sipping café au lait
As if by tasting the flavors of the South of France
I could resurrect her charm, her persona,
Our French mama

The wind has been blowing like the Mistral
Stirring up dust and memories—
The smells, the sounds, those bottles of Tavel wine
The color of the afternoon
You saying "Vous parlez tres bien,"
though our words stumble like runners
on your cobblestone streets

I wonder where you are now
In that sad and gaudy cemetery
on the edge of town,
or walking the gnarled Grenache vines?
Trading stories like old vintages
Perhaps mingling with the sky
on Mount Ventoux's summit?

The wind has been blowing like the Mistral,
and I got the news Madame Mourre died

Old School

Elders don't tweet
Don't need to
Strong voices carry
like thunder across a prairie,
gunshots in city streets
Essential truths
told in tales
handed down
True history

As real as the ghosts
of Emmett Till,
Philando Castille,
George Floyd

Twitterings and postings—
online lies
melt into their own cesspools
in the face of a real mama speaking

Which begs the question:
Where are the mamas
of liars and pretenders
and wimp-ass politicians?
Where are those mamas
layin' down what is
and what shall be?
Where are those strong voices?
Surely everyone has a mama?
Come on out mamas
Come quick!

Queen Street Dublin: A Short Story

A man, a woman, both thirty-something,
sit in a Thai restaurant with their son
Son looks about seven
Man sits next to boy
Woman sits across from son
They order
Woman texts on cell phone
Man sits
Boy sits
Boy has noodles
Woman, small plate—salad?
Man, huge mound—rice? noodles?
Woman still texts
Man says nothing
Boy slurps up noodles
Man and Woman don't eat
Woman gets up
Man gets up
They are gone a long time

"Something is bad," thinks the boy
More bad than when he broke
mama's Blue Willow teacup
More bad than when he lied
about two pages of homework
not done

Boy picks at his food
Watches the door
Man and woman come back in
She sits, he sits
Nobody talks

Social Studies

Boy nibbles another noodle
Woman texts, eats a leaf
Man sits like heart-broken Buddha
Dinner getting cold

If Only, or (Un) Intended Consequences

If only she weren't so sensitive
So aware
If only she could become ostrich
Head in sand
Unseeing unhearing
If only
it would be OK.

But it's not
If only she sees, hears, feels
The world crumbling away
She knows it's a hearing
A vote away
Rights that were hers
Disappear in front of her unbelieving eyes
That other Homo Sapiens
Would make her life illegal
Would make her concerns
An entry in the lawbooks

Out her window
She sees the earth storming
Like her, fighting for life
Fires, floods, hurricanes
The world shudders upon itself

She sees men with guns
Senselessly take away
Fathers and mothers
Brothers and sisters
She hears their screams and wailing
Feels the hatred

Social Studies

If only...
If only...
And then she realizes
Her only If only

Is if she adds
Her spirit
To the many spirits
That are God

Ode to Mary Oliver
9-10-1935 – 1-17-2019

The Snowy Owl
Glides, you can't say "flies"
That implies the sound of feathers
In the wind
The beat of wings

A field mouse, startled
Wonders it has not
Felt the grasp of talons

The owl is not hunting
It is taking it all in
The racket of pounding heartbeat
The texture of winter bluestem
January thaw puddling in backyards
Snow reflecting a galaxy of gibbous moons
The scent of storm
Descending the Cascades
That will blow in
Tomorrow night at eleven

The Snowy Owl
Commits all to memory
Transformation to spirit
A Mary Oliver poem

Mary Becomes the Evening

Mary Ziegenhagen 1938 - 2020

Five o'clock Pacific Time
Saturday afternoon
in the wine country,
still bright in spring light,
Mary becomes the sky

We do not know yet
here in Minnesota,
but sense a shift in the breeze
Mary enters our house,
our lungs, our beings

We stretch up from chairs
Spines stronger
Shoulders back
A twinkling memory—
Baskets of bread,
glasses of Sonoma Cabernet
and words, words, words
shared around laden tables

Now, primed for the news,
we repose into the evening
full of spirit,
full of sky

Au Revoir

Brewster Chamberlin 1939 -2020

The physical form of Brewster fades
but his spirit abounds
The air full of stories
echoing from places his soul has marked—
The evenings on Madame Mourre's garage-top
terrace;
The sad and gaudy cemetery in Tavel;
The stone wall at Uzes;
Burgers at O'Gara's in St. Paul
In D. C.—
The Eastern Market,
The Holocaust Museum,
The Hawk and Dove
And Corfu, Germany,
Key West

All these places
Brewster inhabits
with his knowing chuckle;
a muttered "D'accord",
"Eh, bien"

And the writing!
His memoir *The Time in Tavel—a sojourn in
Provence—*
documenting the time and place where we met
And of course, his poetry *—Situation Reports on the
Emotional Equipoise*
Even his own obituary a prose poem, an historical
document,

Social Studies

so that now
Brewster, faded in body
bounces in our brains
Not "au revoir",
but "bienvenue"

Our Johnny, We Hardly Knew Ye

John Steward 1945-2021

We know our histories together around the dinner
table:
wine, the communion of ideas,
our conversation heightened with you raising questions:
"Why spend the State surplus on tax rebates?"
"Why not early voting by mail?"
How deftly you opposed our pe-conceived notions
and hasty judgements

But lately,
we do not know your thoughts, deep and restless
What did we miss?
What insight prodding with lights turned up?

Your forceful but gentle voice
is mute,
yet still stirs
in the air around us
Come on John,
enlighten us

Night Wanderings

Dad is looking for his mother
Can't blame him
The long road down is not the road
he wants to travel alone
What better companion
than Mother
even if she is a spirit—a whisper
She is still a comfort

If only he could find her
Wandering hallways of early morning
Dad catches a glimpse
echoes bouncing 'round his brain
He calls, "Ume, Ume, is that you?"

First Fall, January 2019

The weather warning sent us packing—
An early New Year's celebration
fortuitous and perhaps foreshadowing;
we arrive at home to learn Dad fell

"No big deal," he says. "Just a bump
No problem."
But we see the slope now
We watch more closely his walk

We become Mom:
"Don't forget this or that
Do this, do that"
Check his meds
Leave Post-its for the nursing staff

I hear him reply "No worries"
Maybe he doesn't,
but more and more
we measure the angle of the slope

Even as it varies
by a half degree of pitch,
Claudia and I wake too early,
go to sleep too late

The Second Fall...

...brings the ubiquitous black walker—
semi-deluxe, with fold up seat,
and hand brakes;
a secret compartment
where Dad hides all the bills
until I check—past due

Designed for when his legs give out,
he can just sit
and scootch along;
foot propelled
like Fred Flintstone

The second fall brings a slight list to port—
a sailor's walk,
tilted forward
as if to keep himself propelled
And propel he does;
buzzing along,
his four-cylinder hitting high revs,
I quicken my pace to keep up

The Valley Path

Dad, you have been on this path
longer than you know
and surely longer than I know
with my myopic sight
The slope so slight at first
you cannot detect the decline
Subtle signs
"What did I have for lunch?"
"Who was just here?"
"Why is there popcorn on the floor?"

Then, a stubbed toe on the rocky path
Into bushes (Hawthorn? Sumac?)
You stop, brush off the dust,
press on
Slower now.
looking for a stout windfall—
oak or maple preferred
to steady your gait
and break the pace
The path angles more steeply
the toe stubbing pebbles
become knee gashing outcrops

You will fall and fall again
each time harder to get up
each time the path falls away
more sharply

Until the last fall
you do not get up
but are carried back to the path

Social Studies

you feel the motion
rolling and breaking
rolling and breaking

You feel my hand grasping yours
Rubbing your fingers and feet
I kiss your forehead
Say "I will be here"
But you know in your heart
and soul
I cannot follow this path

And at last
the pathway evens out
no rolling bed,
no rails or encumbrances
You stand
on your own
the pathway lost in mist
only a doorway
Tentative at first,
and then with resolve
you turn the doorknob,
pull,
step over the threshold

FUTURE HISTORIES

In Japanese culture, (and in many other cultures), a mentor traditionally includes the work of protegees as part of their own work—a way of introducing the next generation of artists and writers. What follows is the work of former students of mine who responded to a request for writing. The students retain the copyright to their writing. I hope you will see some of these poems as part of their own collections!

Social Studies

Failure

ANUJ PRIYADARSHI

Always there
Never leaves
Whenever it reveals itself,
it will shoot your confidence
You worry about it too much

I know I do
It can be a simple mistake
It can be letting someone down
It can be a feeling
It might be losing

You try and fight it
Covering it up
You work off of it
It can help you
It can hurt
From the inside out

It may contain you
While you try and fix it
With all your effort
And heart too

You try and push it away
But it keeps coming back
Each time stronger than before
With more might
And meaning
You try your best
And yet it creeps its way in

You battle against it
You try not to have it
But maybe one day
It will battle for you

Grandma

ANUJ PRIYADARSHI

She is the most kind-hearted person in the world
She lives to please my family
She takes stress off of me, my brother, my mother
and my father
So selflessly (GOD GRANDMA LEAVE SOME PAIN
FOR US)
She takes the stress and keeps it
I wish that one day she could just ball all of her
negative thoughts
And all her stress
Anything that makes her unhappy, and just put it
into a vault and
destroy that vault

She is a warrior who is respected
She is a person who can be strict and firm and yet
somehow be so soft
and gentle
She has an unsustainable amount of knowledge in
her head
She is my grandma
Not yours
Get your own personal GODDESS!

The Painful Truth

DASHA KOVDIY

Death was wandering around the forest
Trying his best
to act fine after seeing the pain
of the loved ones
he had put to rest

Life was there too
From birds to deer
You could see in their souls
There was no fear

There was no fear
Just living their life
until they saw death coming
with his blood-curdling knife

Confused, life followed death
Why were they scared?
What will he do?
Where will he go?
Is it someone they knew?

Death turned around
seeing life following him
Not caring, he kept walking in shame
And his sad-looking grin

Life asked,
"Why do people love me and hate you?"
Death replied
"Because you are the beautiful lie and I am the
painful truth."

The Art and Science of Humanity

HANNAH BECRAFT

Experiment #1
Hypothesis: Every human can be related to a single
flower if one tries hard enough
Reasoning: Humans are simple; easy to understand
Duration: 365 days

Experiments #35
He smiles like sunbeams on Saturday
In the back of your brain, you know it'll be there
But it's still surprising as it spreads its warmth all over
He grows sunflowers out of his footsteps
They're bold and bright and tall
It's a yellow you can't ignore
The kind that makes the edges of your lips pull back

He smells like Strawberry Chapstick
Like the one that sits at the bottom of my backpack
It's a bittersweet scent that always finds its way to
your nose

I painted murals of sunflowers day and night
So many I think petals began to fall from my mouth
And yellow was permanently painted into my fingernails

He smiles like sunbeams on Saturday
He grows flowers out of his footsteps
He smells like Strawberry Chapstick

I painted murals of sunflowers day and night
Until the color yellow was so overwhelming
That it made me sick to my stomach

Until it was all I saw and all I dreamt of
And I couldn't see my hands behind all the paint

Until the color yellow was all the world.

He smiles like sunbeams on Saturday
He grows flowers out of his footsteps
He smells like Strawberry Chapstick

Experiment #71

And I painted murals of sunflowers until I didn't
know who I was anymore.
Until the petals started to taste sour.

Experiment #103

I spent 365 days relating human beings to flowers
It was a science experiment gone wrong
Or maybe just a product of my own deluded fantasies
Painting watercolor words on blank canvases
Humans are simple
Aren't we all just flowers in the end?

I compared the wavelengths of our souls
Nights were spent studying the diagrams of sunflowers
And trying to find the correlation to you
Outlined in Crayola
You somehow always spill over the edges
Getting watercolor where it shouldn't be
But I was convinced it should

There were not enough coffee dates with java chip
frappuccinos
And lovely handholds in the world

Social Studies

To make me feel the way you do
And in the end wasn't that the problem?
In the end
When I was convinced I was nothing but a bitter
storm
Of confusion and rage and colorless grey
And I asked every night
How unfair
How unfair it is that I was nothing but a shipwreck
While you danced through life
And through others' brains.

And I am clutching onto vivid memories
Painting myself daily in an attempt to bring back
who I once was

Because you never meant it
'Least not the way I meant it.

Experiment #177
I am sick and I do not know who I am
I am afraid
Within the depersonalized haze
The scent of espresso and stale bread
Is mixed with that of sweat and Strawberry Chapstick
I will have you know

I haven't been able to look at Strawberry Chapstick
since you
I am sick and I do not know who I am
It seems lately the moon has loved me too much
And kept me awake for almost all hours of her reign
I am sick and I am tired
Lately it feels like I am tired all the time.

I painted mural of sunflowers day and night
There are 26 paintings hanging in my attic

I am begging you to let me go.
Pure adoration hurts too much
And my heart was not built for that.

Experiment #202
My house is covered in yellow pixie dust
Your yellow pixie dust
And I am scrubbing desperately
I am staring in horror at the bright color
And trying to breathe
There is nothing more terrifying than yellow suffo-
cation
And I am scrubbing desperately
I am begging you to let me go.

Experiment #253
I flew to another country
It was a desperate attempt to obtain fresh air
I flew to another country
A desperate attempt to feel my soul at peace again
I flew to another country
To stop feeling the weight of the grey watercolor
Of every bridge I burned
I burned them all in a month.

So, I traveled 6,765.3 miles
Spent over 24 hours on planes.
And finally
The thought of you was not looming over me
I was not being swarmed by shadows
That reeked of fear and smoke and blood

Social Studies

I was not staying up all night to outline delicate
flowers
And flood them full of the color of you
I was not sick and I was starting to figure out who I was.

Experiment #328
Tell me why there were burnt flowers on my porch
Tell me why those canvases I'd thrown out are back
There are 62 painted canvases in my attic
62
62 times I was so overwhelmed and stained with
yellow paint
62 times I wished I wasn't.

He smiles like sunbeams on Saturday
He grows sunflowers out of his footsteps
He smells like Strawberry Chapstick

But I guess we might as well make it 63.

Experiment # 341
There are 62 painted canvases in my attic

He smiles like sunbeams on Saturday
He grows sunflowers out of his footsteps
He smells like Strawberry Chapstick
He is a liar.

He spread honey on his hands
And watched as we all flocked around him
Eager and starry eyed

He grows dandelions out of his footsteps
And maybe we were all too blind to notice.

Experiment #365

He has left his fingerprints on everything I own
And yet he never stepped foot here.

I am learning the process now

Relearning how to spend my day without him.
I cleared out my garden,
I don't grow sunflowers here anymore.

I am learning how to process now.
I am learning how to be human now.

I spent 365 days equating humans to flowers
I painted murals of sunflowers day and night
And I swore he smelled like Strawberry Chapstick.
When I saw those burnt sunflowers
I was reminded of every mistake I made before.

Humans are simple
Aren't we all flowers in the end?
I spent 365 days trying to prove that

But I am learning how to process now.

I cleared out my garden,
I have decided to grow a forest for myself.

Experiment #382

I spent 365 days relating humans to flowers
But humans are not simple.

There are approximately 0 painted canvases in my attic
There are approximately 0 sunflowers in my garden.

Social Studies

I am learning how to process now

With every helping hand she gives
I am remembering how to be human now

I have smiled more times in the past month,
Than I did throughout the duration of my experiment.
I know that as she smiles at me
The sense of reassurance
I am letting deep breaths travel through my veins
Coloring me with my natural skin tone
Filling my anxious ribcage with hope and love.

I am remembering how to process now
Humans are not simple
People are not flowers
And I am remembering how to be human now.

Soup

JANELLE TABAKOV

Cooking has always been an escape for me
An expression of the soul
Allowing me to think
While creating sustenance
My body oh so craves

How many others like me
Spend hours
Behind a kitchen counter
Transforming farm fresh ingredients
Into a meal fit for a king
Disappearing in an instant
The evidence wiped away
Leaving only a faint aroma

In all honesty
My body can survive
On the few sips of water I allow it
And it will survive on the instant meals
Scavenged from the depth of my freezer
However, I am afraid that my mind will not
So, you must understand when I slip again
I often find myself chopping vegetables
Dissolving bouillon paste
And pouring my legume of choice
Into a well-used pot

Uncertain

JANELLE TABAKOV

Standing in the aisle
She looks at the never-ending mess
Where is her prize
Hiding amongst imposters
Determined, she finds the place she's looking for
Which one will be worthy
Two opponents are picked
One filled with irony
One filled with meaning

Before the choice would be clear
But this situation
It's different

The thought worries her
What will she do
Knowing she's timed her mind races
The words blur
And the colors blend
Everything is a distraction in her decision
Obstacles
She thinks
That's all they are
Don't pay attention
A voice behind her
A warning
"5 minutes left"
The connections she's made with each of the com-
petitors
How will she choose
Is this what betrayal feels like

Time's up
Irony has won
"Good job you picked a birthday card"
My sister says

When I'm Lost

JANELLE TABAKOV

When I'm lost
I find my way back
Yet the pathway is different
Each time

I track my last steps
An explorer some say
I find the stale breadcrumbs
I seem to have never left

I go back to the beginning
And go forward again
One step
Two step

But wait
Where's forward
Where's back
I haven't gone anywhere.
I seem to be lost again
It's just dark
I scream for help
But an echo comes back
Where is the light
Have I strayed from the path
Once again

Just close your eyes and remember
Remember
The light

Lurking in the shadows
I find it
A light
A friend
A hand
And then the path

I'm glad for the adventure
But I've had enough
I like this light
I like this friend.
I like this hand
But maybe some other time

When I was a Butterfly

MIKAELA PAVLICEK_

i was a butterfly from the womb
born with wings for limbs and
nectar dripping dripping dripping
from my lips

carefree: beautiful
an angel floating not flying
unafraid of the falling

and when i was a butterfly
oh god
i was striking and
not afraid to speak loudly

i would not could not be god fearing
for i did not know shame

as i got older
i molded
into a cocoon
i was not aware existed
and i became shy shy shy
shrinking
into my chrysalis

     a child on the monkey bars
hanging- hanging- hanging
a crash landing
oh god
a backwards
metamorphosis

a fat, ugly caterpillar i became
i am not carefree: beautiful

oh god
i am sorry i sucked nectar
from your petals, forbidden & reckless love
please do not abandon me.

i would confess anything to get my wings back
i am praying praying praying
a larva i lay

oh god
are you there?

When He Asks

MIKAELA PAVLICEK

when he asks about my family
i say that

my brother
is the grandfather clock that hangs from the wall,
seeing the world in one big, detailed instruction manual,
he is honest to a fault and rarely wrong.

my brother is the engineer of my family,
a loud reminder that time should not be wasted,
and that we are always late.

and my father
is the animals that follow him into the kitchen each
morning,
eager for breakfast and acknowledgment,
he is their alpha, they are his pack.

my father is the shepherd of the family,
he guides us all home and makes sure that no one
is left behind.

and my mother
yes, my mother is the puzzle that sits on our dining room
table unfinished, a mess waiting to be cleaned up,
she is patient in ways that the rest of us are not.

my mother is the carpenter of our family,
and nothing is ever too broken for her to put back
together.

and what about you?
he asks

i am the poetry of my family
my fingertips callused from typing,
i am every word that i have not yet written.
yet, i am the writer of the family,
hoping that one day my words will become our
legacy.

In Came a Bus From Idaho

MORGAN KERBER-FOLSTROM

As a child, I often stayed with my family in Idaho
I grew up on a reservation
So it was nice to see how a family should flow
I sadly wait in a bus station

But I knew I had to leave
Leave what a family should be like
I'm not that naïve
My own parents are warlike

They argue all the time
They scream and they hit
Living in a house full of grime
Inhaling the smoke their drugs would emit

I jumped onto the Greyhound bus
A fifth-grader all alone
And yet no one made a fuss
I didn't even have a phone

In came a bus from Idaho
I had made it home I was now aware
I paid the driver what I owe
And my parents weren't there

I waited and waited for them to come
And yet mom and dad never did
They didn't care and I felt glum
They never came to pick up their kid
My grandpa eventually came and bent on a knee
They must have forgotten he said with no doubt

FUTURE HISTORIES

I'd be staying with my uncle and aunt he told me
Until my parents figured their lives out

And what came next, I never could have known
Because my parents didn't show
I would stay with my aunt and uncle till I was grown

In came a bus from Idaho

What They Forget About Hubris

MORGAN KERBER-FOLSTROM

It's a bittersweet victory
As the wax sears into his skin
As the sun grows smaller in the sky
And, oddly enough, all he can do is smile

All he can do is grin with pride
For he reached heights no one ever had before
He kissed the sun and although it burned
It tasted like the sweetest fruit on his tongue

The wind flows through his hair
Playing a sick lullaby to accompany his fall
Feathers fly high up in the sky
As his hope falls apart on his back

Icarus resigned himself to this end
But did not go with fear in his heart
His father let out a cry
And he uttered a goodbye to the wind

The sea grew closer
And all he could do was laugh
There is something so beautiful
In falling when you should be flying

Many looked upon his story with pity
Because so many people seem to forget
For those blinded by hubris
The fall is just as exhilarating as the climb

ACKNOWLEDGEMENTS

Writing is not a solo work! This book is the result of the insights, advice and encouragement from many people in my life: My wife, Claudia Daly, has been cheerleader, confidant, advisor and first editor. This book would not be what it is without the generous, wise and artful editing by my friend and co-conspirator, Mary Jo Thompson. Her gentle (but firm) guidance shaped the form and spirit of the work. Unexpected and welcome editing came from writer pals, Sharon Chmielarz and Margaret Hasse—they really fine-tuned this book! Sharon, Margaret, and Jeanne Lutz added their kind words and support, and I am humbled by their graciousness. Thanks to Liz Dwyer for the wonderful layout and book design. Special thanks to James Monroe for the wonderful cover art. Thanks also to the (former) students who responded to my call for poems. It takes courage to put your work out there, and the book is richer and more diverse thanks to your contributions!

Thank you also to the wonderous community of writers who are my cattle prod and my safety net. Special kudos to the League of Minnesota Poets, and its performance wing, Cracked Walnut for giving writers venues to voice their work. I am forever grateful to Donna Isaac who co-founded, hosted, and curated the Literary Bridges Reading Series with me. Independent bookstores are the lifeblood of the writing community—thanks to all of them for their faith and guts! Special shout outs to Next Chapter Booksellers, Subtext, Eat My Words, Irreverent Bookworm and Red Balloon in the Twin Cities; and Zenith in Duluth.

STANLEY KUSUNOKI

is the author of three previous collections of poetry:

Shelter in Place: Poems in a Time of COVID-19;

Items in the News;

and *180 Days: Reflections and Observations of a Teacher.*

He has taught creative writing to young people through programs at The Loft, Asian-American Renaissance, Intermedia Arts, and S.A.S.E., The Write Place. He was a recipient of a Loft Asian-American Inroads mentorship and was awarded a Minnesota State Arts Board Cultural Collaboration grant to create, write, and perform *Beringia, the Land Bridge Project* with Ojibwe performance poet, Jamison Mahto, at Intermedia Arts. Stan was selected as one of 16 writers in the "2023 Featured Authors" program for the Anoka County Library. He is co-host/curator of the Literary Bridges Reading Series at Next Chapter Booksellers in St. Paul. Most recently, Kusunoki was the High Potential Coordinator at Red Oak Elementary School in Shakopee, Minnesota. He lives in St. Paul with his wife, Claudia Daly.